Pro Logo

Logos, products, and
advertising material
for brands illustrating
some of the topics
dealt with in the book

The power of calligraphy

1) Coca-Cola intertwined L and C

© Coca-Cola

© Oriani & Orione – photogroup

2) Bulgari's pointed "U"

Tridimensional emblems

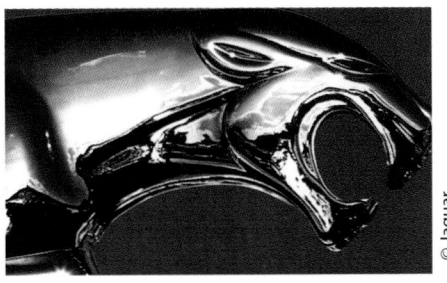

© Jaguar

3) The "Leaper," the hood ornament used on certain Jaguar models, which remains an important part of the brand's identity and is the inspiration for the current two-dimensional logo

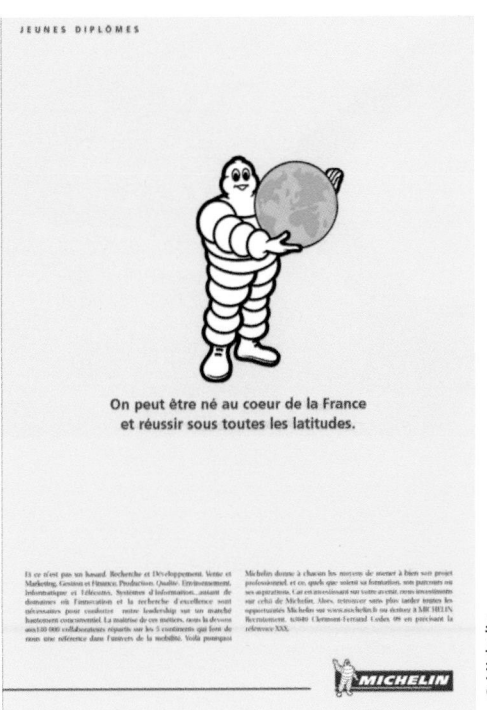

JEUNES DIPLÔMES

On peut être né au coeur de la France
et réussir sous toutes les latitudes.

© Michelin

4) The Michelin logo, considered the world's best known

5) The Renault lozenge is a rare example of a recent logo in 3D

© Renault

Logomania

As trends fluctuate, logo-covered materials periodically come back into fashion.

6) The famous Bally "Busy B", reproduced with permission of Solve Sundsbø, photographer

Logomania (II)

© Christian Dior, Nick Knight

7) At Christian Dior, the return of the mongrammed fabric, in an updated version

Evolution of logos

A constant search for fine adjustment, appropriateness to current tastes,
and modernization, while endeavoring not to weaken awareness of the brand.

1900

1904

1909

1929

1948

1955

1961

1971

1995

1999

8) The more than century-old history of one of the most familiar logos,
the famous Shell "Pecten" with its distinctive yellow and red color

Evolution of logos (II)

The new logos are clearer, simpler, and more modern – in short, a more classical esthetic.

Old

New

© Lanvin

9) Lanvin's

Burberrys OF LONDON

BURBERRY

© Burberry

10) Burberry's

© Lancel

11) Lancel's

A virtual image of women

The canons of beauty espoused by the fashion world promote a figure that is far removed from the morphology of today's women.

Fortunately, brands like The Body Shop, are counteracting this trend and promote values related to naturality. You can see the Ruby doll presented as the anti-Barbie with the slogan: "There are 3 billion women in the world and only 8 top models."

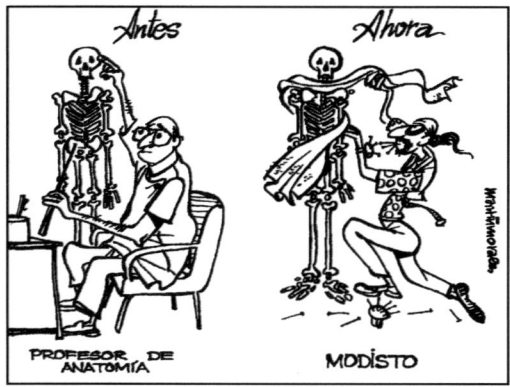

12) Cartoon by Martin Morales
first published in *abc*, March 18, 1999

13) The Body Shop

14) The Body Shop's "Ruby doll"

Provocation

15) Cover page from *Elle* Spain (May 1998) showing what has become an annual theme every May

Provocation (II)

16) Advertising from the Italian firm Diesel which at the outset based its brand identity on provocation

Provocation (III)

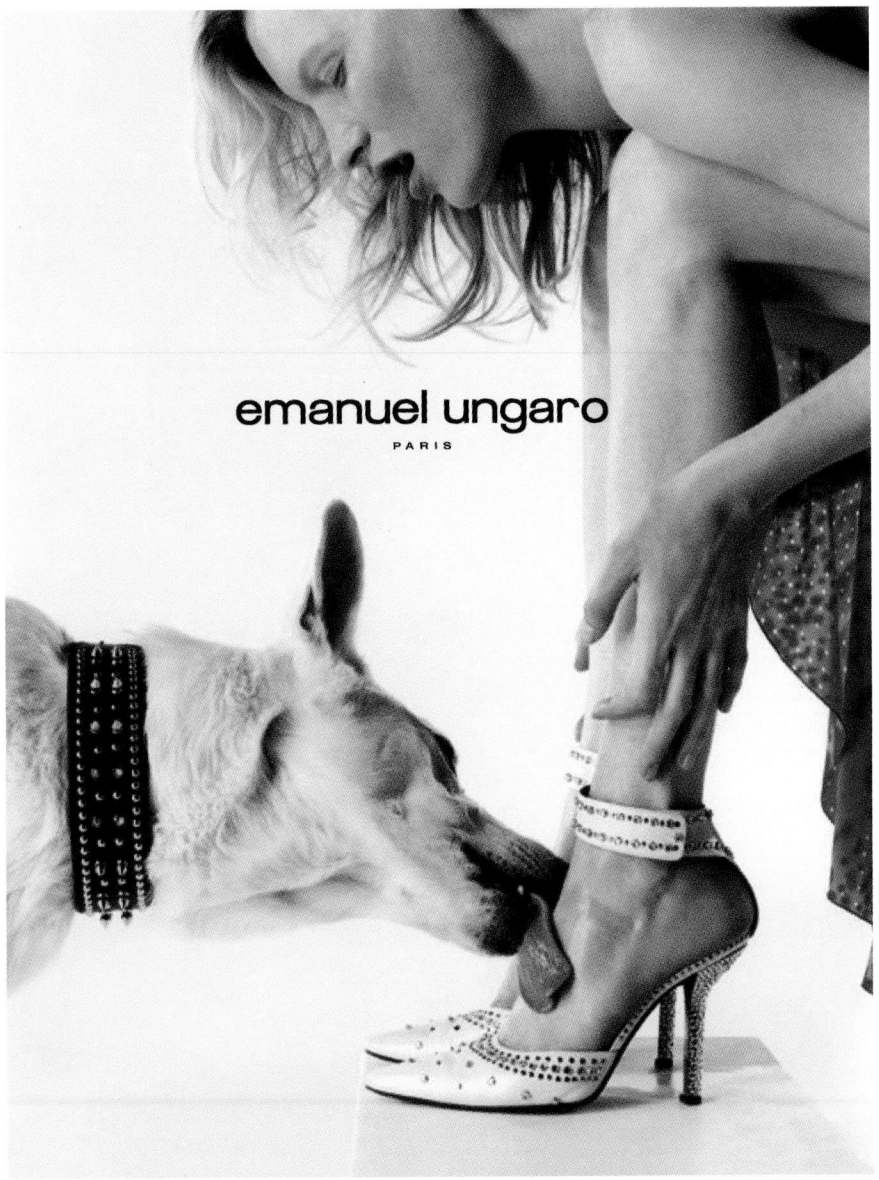

© Ungaro

17) For Ungaro, superb-quality photos – unfortunately using strong provocation with sexual connotations – to promote the inestimable creative talent of one of the last authentic couturiers, who has no need of such artifice

Provocation (IV)

Extract from Sisley campaigns, photographed by Terry Richardson, where the erotic and sexual component is intended to promote a brand identity whose values are supposedly linked to virtual travel and sometimes brutal "pulp" lifestyles.
The products attempt to be in phase with the most avant-garde fashion trends.

© Sisley

18) Sisley campaign 2002: Baroque

© Sisley

19) Sisley campaign 2001: Farming

Provocation (V)

© Sisley

20) Sisley campaign 2000: Manhattan

© Sisley

21) Sisley campaign 2000: Palm Springs

Provocation (VI)

The controversial Benetton campaigns photographed by Oliviero Toscani.

22) Benetton campaign 1992, HIV (David Kirby)

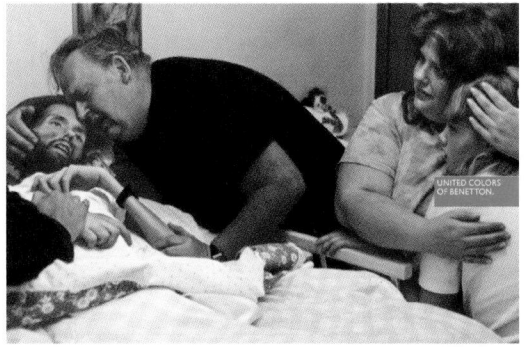

23) Benetton campaign 1996, Hearts

24) Benetton campaign 1994, Bosnian soldier

25) Benetton campaign 1993, HIV frontal

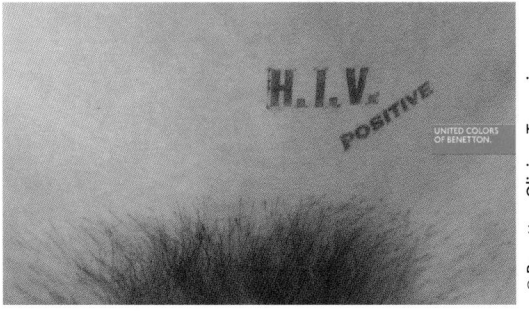

Provocation (VII)

26) Benetton campaign: a priest and nun kissing

27) Benetton campaign Spring 2003, "Food for life" photographed by James Mollison, who continues the "ethical" line instituted by his predecessor Oliviero Toscani

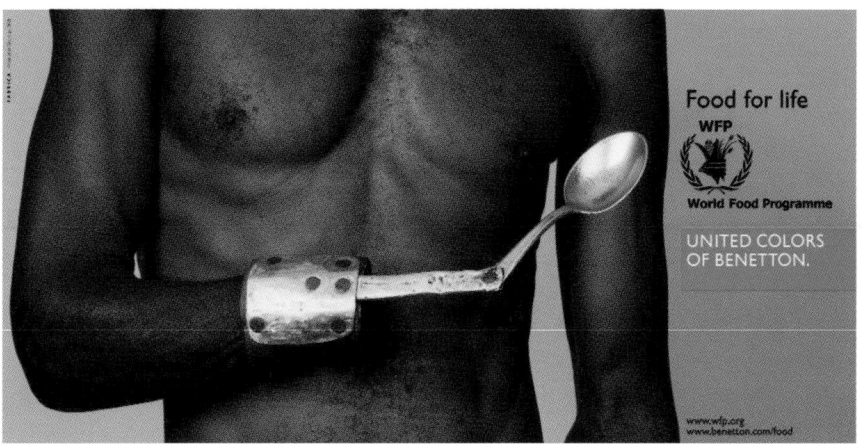

Profaning the sacred

28) Power is useless without control: the famous Pirelli ad showing soccer star Ronaldo wearing an Inter Milan jersey and overlooking Guanabara Bay, in imitation of the pose of the Christ of Corcovado statue in Rio de Janiero

Commercializing values of solidarity

© Kenneth Cole

29) Kenneth Cole continues the moralizing announcements on which he has based his campaigns. Here, the brand declares, "On September 12 (2001), people who don't talk to their parents forgot why"

© Kenneth Cole

30) Kenneth Cole December 1999 campaign, on the Worldwide Day Against AIDS

© Fortuna

31) The Fortuna cigarette brand announces, "Helping doesn't cost so much" and donates 0.7% of the purchase price to charities

A few good ads

32) "No female body was exploited in making this advertisement"
Eram treats a current theme with humor and originality while still spotlighting the product

A few good ads (II)

33) Lightware: again humor and wit to address prevailing consumer concerns

A few good ads (III)

34) "Ducati people 2002" campaign which shows authentic "Ducatisti,"
highlighting the emotional nature of the link between consumers and the mythical brand

A few good ads (IV)

35) Superb handling of modernity and tradition, with esthetic sensibility. Rosemary Bravo, Burberry CEO, resolves the eternal dilemma of luxury brands

© Burberry

Managing a brand's esthetic

Two examples of changing a logo in the banking sector

Old

New

36) Banco Sabadell logos

Old

New Crédit du Nord ★

37) Crédit du Nord logos

Managing a brand's esthetic (II)

A few logos of Swiss brands, all in red and white.
There are many other Swiss brands that use their national colors.

38) White on red square for Bally …

39) and the same for Swiss International Air Lines, both expressing their Swiss nationality

40) Mondaine

41) Tissot

42) Swatch

Three examples of watch brands using the white cross on a red background, a frequent practice in many Swiss economic sectors

Managing a brand's esthetic (III)

OUR SWISSNESS

The new airline has a powerful brand heritage that will propel it forward. The past success and status of the legend stem from its Swiss origin and it is this dedication to "Swissness" that will define the future.

There are a number of values common to Swiss International Air Lines and Crossair which mirror the values of Switzerland: quality, prestige, tradition in care, service, efficiency, security, reliability, cleanliness and Swiss heritage.

Universally accepted and well-respected, these Swiss values will be coveted by consumers looking for a superior travel experience.

43) Extract from "A short story about civilized aviation," developed by
the new Swiss International Air Lines to promote and explain its new identity

Managing a brand's esthetic (IV)

classical and baroque esthetics

© Ducados, Maria Espeus

44) Advertisement for Spanish Ducados cigarettes, with a classical page layout and a baroque photo, using "clair-obscur" lighting techniques and framing to suggest the atmosphere of the tango bars of Cuba and Buenos Aires

45) Another baroque advertisement for Ducados

46) Versace's famous baroque cushion

© Versace

© Ducados, Maria Espeus

Managing a brand's esthetic (V)

classical and baroque esthetics (II)

47) Superb baroque photo for the American brand Guess

© Chanel

Managing a brand's esthetic (VI)

classical and baroque esthetics (III)

48) Chanel's baroque photograph for the most classical perfume bottle

Salvatore Ferragamo

© Salvatore Ferragamo

Managing a brand's esthetic (VII)

classical and baroque esthetics (IV)

49) A typical classical photograph for Ferragamo's Spring 2003 campaign:
white background and incredibly clear details of the stitching and of the leather
on their proprietory wedge heel

Managing a brand's esthetic (VIII)

classical and baroque esthetics (V)

50) Classical Ferragamo shoes with the baroque label created by the founder Salvatore

© Salvatore Ferragamo

© Chanel

51) Classical Chanel photography for another classical bottle

© Lancel

52) Lancel's former classical logo

What do you look for in a great pair of jeans?

They should have just the right amount of
give and take, let you move easily

and fit like your favorite pair, only better.

Look for jeans with a touch of LYCRA®.

You'll live in 'em.

Enjoy The Difference™
www.LYCRA.com

© Lycra

Managing a brand's esthetic (IX)

classical and baroque esthetics (VI)

53) A fine classical photo for Lycra, one of the rare fabric brands that addresses consumers directly

Example of diversification

54) Pirelli is known primarily for its tires, though it is active in many other industrial areas, such as fiber optics. The company created a new brand, "P zero", which uses the calligraphy of its famous "P," and in the case of the shoes, a tire-tread design on the synthetic soles. If you can put tires on cars, why not shoes on feet?

Restyling in the automotive industry

55) The Volkswagen Beetle's stylistic evolution from 1955 to 1998

© Volkswagen

© BMW

56) Old and new Mini Cooper from Morris

Straightforward expression of the ethical values underlying the brand identity

57) No need for a sophisticated semiotic analysis to perceive and understand the ethical values expressed by the Mecca-Cola brand

© Mecca-Cola